Contents

Introduction

Jiu jitsu is a Japanese expression meaning 'compliant art'. This curious title arises because classical jiu jitsu techniques use the opponent's strength against him. The opponent pushes, but instead of pushing back you go along with – 'comply' with – him and pull him towards you. Using force in this way means not having to rely on superior strength to win.

Jiu jitsu makes use of strikes and kicks to divert the opponent, throws to unbalance him, hold downs to keep him immobile, and locks to control him through leverage applied to the joints. It also teaches the counter movements to all these various attacks, so you will learn how to block the opponent's punches and kicks, how to prevent him from throwing you, and how to escape from locks and hold downs.

The origins of jiu jitsu lie far back in the past and there is no clear line of historical development – it seems to be involved with just about every martial art practised in Japan. For example, the ancient histories of Japanese wrestling (*Sumo*) and jiu jitsu are so closely linked that it is difficult to tell where one ends and the other begins. Jiu jitsu is also associated with the techniques of Japanese swordplay (*Kenjutsu*) because some of these required the warrior to close with and disarm the opponent. The infamous Japanese secret warriors known as the *Ninja* used jiu jitsu techniques as part of their own fighting system, while the founders of aikido and shorinji kempo were both jiu jitsu masters. In more recent times, one of the four major schools of karate was founded by a teacher of jiu jitsu.

Jiu jitsu is not only associated with Japanese martial arts. We know, for example, that some jiu jitsu techniques come from China because history tells us that the Southern Shaolin boxer Chin Gempin taught kung fu techniques to Japanese warriors. Some of the striking techniques he taught came to be known as *Kempo* and you may still see this name associated with jiu jitsu practice.

Though jiu jitsu has its origins far back in history, it is alive and developing in the present day. As society and circumstances have changed, so jiu jitsu has adapted to meet new challenges.

The jiu jitsu taught within the World Jiu Jitsu Federation comes from the whole world of martial practice, from classical weapons work to modern and effective self defence systems. So whether you are interested in the martial art of past centuries, or in something that works in the present day, jiu jitsu will fit the bill. No other martial art can offer such a wide range of techniques and applications.

However, the road to excellence in jiu jitsu practice is a long and hard one which makes great demands on both the body and mind of the student. Physical fitness comes through practice but mental fitness is sometimes harder to develop. First of all, jiu jitsu practice calls for patience and persistence – to keep working at techniques until they are right. Secondly, jiu jitsu demands a true humility which comes about only through self knowledge. By all means be moderately pleased with yourself for reaching the standard you hold, but never be envious or contemptuous about the standard of others. Thirdly, jiu jitsu requires students to have an enquiring mind that looks closely at what is being taught. Don't be content merely to copy, understand as well because knowledge allows you to develop your practice.

Acknowledgements
Thanks to David Mitchell for his help with the text, and to Alan Campbell for taking part in the demonstrations.
Photography by Martin Sellars.

Note Throughout the book jiu jitsu students are referred to individually as 'he'. This should, of course, be taken to mean 'he or she' where appropriate.

The World Jiu Jitsu Federation

The World Jiu Jitsu Federation (WJJF) represents the culmination of 30 years' jiu jitsu and general martial art experience. That is, three decades of study, development and refinement both in jiu jitsu techniques and in the methods of teaching them. The WJJF was founded in 1976 and its President is Spartaco Bertoletti of Italy. Chief International Technical Director is Robert Clark, the author of this book.

The WJJF is totally committed to the art of jiu jitsu, to its continuing technical development and to teaching the art to anyone willing to learn. There are no exceptions to these commitments! From children and teenagers to elderly people and those with physical disabilities, the WJJF opens its doors to all. Whether you are looking to improve your martial skills, seeking a truly effective self defence system, or trying to increase your awareness and self confidence, the WJJF can meet your needs.

Choosing your club

Choosing the correct jiu jitsu club is the most important step you will take in your training career. Pick the wrong one and you could waste many years of hard practice, because not all jiu jitsu clubs are good clubs! Sadly there is no legal requirement for jiu jitsu instructors to be recognised by a competent national body, and only a few black belts are properly trained coaches.

If you are not already a member of the WJJF, then discover the location of your nearest club by using the address given on page 47. If you are already practising in a jiu jitsu club, then check it is a member of the WJJF by asking the coach whether he is registered with the Federation.

All member clubs of the WJJF register their individual students with the Federation on an annual basis and this means you will receive a WJJF 'licence'. The licence is a receipt for the money you paid for registration; if it does not mention the WJJF, then you have not joined a member club!

The WJJF licence contains a valuable insurance policy that not only protects you from the legal consequences of injuring another student, it also covers yourself against injury and compensates you for the period you are injured. It is therefore essential that you maintain an up-to-date registration by handing in your application form to the club coach **before** your present registration expires.

The licence comes in a Budo pass book which serves to record your personal progress within the WJJF. Don't worry about insurance during those first 31 days because if you paid your fee immediately on joining, then the instructor will have notified WJJF HQ and you will be covered.

Whatever you do, make sure you pay your fee immediately on joining because accidents tend to happen more frequently in the early days of training. That is when you need your insurance the most.

Each time you train, you may be required to pay a mat fee. This varies from club to club. The average length of a session is 90 minutes. It is best to train at least twice a week.

Clothing

It is not necessary to buy a training uniform immediately – a T-shirt and pair of tracksuit bottoms will be fine. At some stage, however, you will want to buy a proper WJJF training tunic.

The distinctive WJJF uniform is of known standard, quality and appearance (fig. 1). If looked after, if will last for several years of hard practice. Buy one that is a size too large because it will shrink slightly with subsequent washings. Wash the tunic every week, otherwise it will quickly become unpleasant both for you and your partner. Remember, a tidy appearance shows self respect and the correct attitude to training; a dirty or ripped suit indicates an uncaring attitude.

Each new tunic is supplied with a belt. Check and see that it is the right colour for your grade. If not, then buy a belt from the club coach. Don't be tempted to dye your old belt. The perspiration produced during training always causes the dye to run and ruin your tunic.

There is a right and a wrong way to tie a belt. Start by wrapping the belt twice around your waist and draw the ends to equal length. Tuck one end up the inside of both coils and bring it over the top. Then bring the second end across and tuck the first under and through, pulling the knot tight.

Tracksuits and flip-flop sandals are useful, especially when you are obliged to walk between the changing room and the practice area. Again, standard tracksuits and flip-flops are available through the club coach and are worth considering because of their high standard.

Fig. 1 WJJF uniform ▶

Grading

Jiu jitsu skills are learned through a ladder of progression known as a grading system. The grading system measures your progress and indicates the level of skill you have reached by means of coloured belts, certificates and entries in your Budo pass (fig. 2). The following colour schemes and minimum grading intervals are used in the WJJF.

- Red to white belt   16 sessions
- White to yellow belt   24 sessions
- Yellow to orange belt   16 sessions
- Orange to green belt   16 sessions
- Green to blue belt   24 sessions
- Blue to purple belt   24 sessions
- Purple to brown belt   36 sessions
- Brown to 1st dan black belt   96 sessions
- 1st to 2nd dan black belt   2 years
- 2nd to 3rd dan black belt   3 years
- 3rd to 4th dan black belt   4 years

(Sometimes the orange belt grade is omitted from the syllabus.)

In addition to the time requirement, students of up to purple belt grade must attend at least one special course each year. These courses are intended both to cover specialist areas of development and to promote friendship between WJJF students from different clubs. Brown belts attempting black belt must attend two such courses each year.

Grading examinations are conducted by the National Coach, or by his appointed examiners. Coloured belt gradings can take place in your club or at a regional centre, but all dan gradings are held at the WJJF's Headquarters.

In order to take your next grading, you must have:

- completed the required number of training sessions
- completed the required number of special courses
- a current WJJF registration
- the correct number and type of badges such that: white belt – WJJF chest badge; yellow belt – chest badge and back patch; orange belt – chest badge, back patch and arm badge; green belt – chest badge, back patch and two arm badges; blue belt and above – chest badge, back patch, two arm badges and two leg flashes.

▲ *Fig. 2 Certificates, belt, Budo pass*

Etiquette and WJJF rules

Etiquette

Jiu jitsu practice begins and ends with courtesy. If you do not respect your teacher, then how can you have respect for yourself for learning under him? If you do not respect your fellow students, how can you expect them to train safely and effectively with you?

Insistence on just one type of jiu jitsu uniform and badges ensures that no social distinctions creep into the training hall. Everyone looks the same and everyone is treated the same – with courtesy. Not only is this courtesy expressed in the form of polite attention to what the teacher is saying, it is also expressed by means of the bow.

When no-one is in the training hall as you enter, pause at the entrance and face the centre of the room. Put your heels together and your hands flat against the front of your thighs. This posture is known as 'attention stance'.

Then perform a standing bow (fig. 3). If other people are in the training hall, then bow towards the senior grade.

Don't bow too far, just incline your upper body forwards. Make the bow smooth. Hesitate at the lowest point for a count of two before straightening up again. As befits the follower of any true fighting art, you should always be on the lookout for attack – so never look down at the floor as you bow.

Once you have made the bow, you can step into the training hall.

Bow also when leaving the hall, even if this is only for a short interval.

The class is called together by a senior member and arranges itself into lines according to grade. Training tunics are adjusted until they are tidy and the following ritual takes place when activity has died down.

Fig. 3 Standing bow ▶

- Begin by standing in attention stance.
- Keep your back straight as you lower your left knee to the mat.
- Lower your right knee and sit back on your calves. Your ankles are now fully extended, so the feet are pointing forwards. Ankle flexibility is the limiting factor in this position and you may need to do some 'homework', perhaps by kneeling on cushions over gradually longer periods until you can hold the position.
- Slide your hands forwards and palm-downwards on to the mat. Bend your elbows and lean forwards in a smooth movement, but keep your eyes on the coach – don't look down at the mat! (*See* fig. 4.)
- Pause at the lowest point, then return smoothly to a straight-back position.
- Return to a standing position by first raising the left knee, then the right. Stand with your feet together once more and perform a standing bow to the coach.

If you miss the opening ritual described above, then pause at the door of the training hall and wait for the coach to call you on to the mat. Go through your warm-up exercises quietly in a corner of the room and then perform the kneeling bow. Remain in the kneeling position and await the coach's invitation to join the lesson.

Pay close attention when the coach is speaking and don't lounge against walls or sprawl over the mat. When the coach is showing the class a technique, make sure you can see the demonstration clearly. Ask questions when the coach invites you to, otherwise do not interrupt. If you are chosen to assist the coach, don't make fatuous remarks or move about without permission. If for any reason you are told to sit down at the side of the mat, tuck your feet under you so that they don't pose an obstruction. Don't discuss techniques loudly with your partner and only practise what you have been shown.

WJJF clubs train on a matted surface. Under no circumstances should you or your guest(s) walk on the mat with shoes on! Walk around the edge of the mat, or leave your shoes at the entrance to the training hall. Do not smoke, eat, or talk noisily.

Jiu jitsu practice involves working in close proximity with another person, so personal hygiene is very important. Tie long hair back with an elastic band because hair grips and metal clasps are dangerous. Ear-rings, necklaces and all other jewellery must be removed and stored safely for the duration of the lesson. Spectacles must not be worn, although you can wear soft contact lenses at your own risk. Keep your finger-nails and toe-nails short.

▲ *Fig. 4 Opening ritual*

WJJF rules

Read and memorise the following regulations since they are standard in WJJF training halls all over the world.

(1) The coach is concerned with your safety and with the correct performance of technique. Obey his directions at all times.

(2) Students may enter and leave the training hall only with the coach's permission.

(3) Instruction may only take place under the direct supervision of a properly qualified WJJF coach. Only currently enrolled members may receive tuition.

(4) Gradings may only take place under the direction of the National Coach of the WJJF or his delegated nominees.

(5) Strangle or sleeper holds must not be practised except under the direct supervision of the coach.

(6) Members of the WJJF must not misuse their knowledge of jiu jitsu.

(7) Jiu jitsu techniques must not be demonstrated outside of a training hall.

(8) Members of the WJJF may not participate in any display of jiu jitsu without prior permission from the WJJF.

(9) Smoking is not allowed in any WJJF training hall.

(10) Outdoor shoes must not be worn in the training hall.

(11) All injuries, whether brought to or incurred during a session, must be reported to the club coach.

(12) The WJJF reserves the right to terminate the membership of any person that the WJJF considers unsuitable for martial art training.

(13) Violation of any of these rules renders a member liable to disciplinary procedures, which may include expulsion from the WJJF.

Training safety

Jiu jitsu can be a strenuous activity, especially for someone coming to it 'cold' from a sedentary job. So check whether you're fit enough to practise. This is particularly important for novices over the age of 40.

Let the coach know of any health conditrons you may have at the time of your application for membership, or as soon as the conditions are diagnosed, whichever is the sooner. Telling the coach this allows him to monitor your performance; he may spot the onset of symptoms before you do.

A health condition could mean epilepsy, migraines, asthma, heart problems, or blood-clotting disorders. Haemophilia is the only health condition that positively disbars you (for your own safety!) from practising the jiu jitsu described in this syllabus. Consult your doctor if you are unaware whether you have a health condition that ought to be disclosed to the coach.

Don't train soon after eating a large meal. This is because the process of digestion uses up a considerable amount of blood which is otherwise required by the exercising muscles – including the heart – and cramp may result.

Certain types of viral infection can have serious side effects on heart muscle, so avoid sharp bangs on the chest and sudden training spurts if you have a cold.

Don't train too close to unshielded windows, glass doors, benches, pillars, or the edge of the mat. Make sure your partner has a clear landing space before you throw him. Take extra care if you are larger than your partner because big people generate a great deal of power without being aware of it. Finally, don't leave training bags or unused kit where they can be tripped over.

Warming up and cooling down

Jiu jitsu is a healthy activity which through its regular practice generates a whole-body fitness characterised by the ability to train for long periods under light loads, to act explosively when circumstances require it, and to move with agility. Jiu jitsu makes no great demands in terms of joint flexibility and neither does it require students to work at near maximum effort over long periods of time. Consequently, there is little need for the long warm-up, cool-down and body preparation programmes found in other martial arts.

Jiu jitsu stresses the notion of 'health'; that is, the whole body and mind working efficiently and in harmony. Jiu jitsu exercises work the body gently and thoroughly, and always well within its limits. Only a small number of such exercises are required to prepare the body and mind for practice, and the most suitable for jiu jitsu practice come from the Far East.

You will note that all except one of the following exercises concentrate on working the spine. This is because the spine has a crucial role in jiu jitsu practice. It does, after all, hold the body upright and all limb actions are transmitted through it or to it. For this reason the spine should be both strong and flexible.

Perform each exercise in a gentle manner, holding it for at least ten seconds at the point of maximum stretch. Avoid all jerky movements and don't cheat! The exercises are not set out in any particular order, so vary them as you please. Concentrate on what you are doing since this mental discipline forms a part of preparing the mind and body for training.

● Lie on your back and bend your knees. Take hold of your ankles and arch your body upwards until only the soles of your feet and the top of your head are supporting your body. Note how the muscles of the chest, abdomen and thighs are stretched. Try to hold this arched position for at least ten seconds, or longer if you can manage it.

● This exercise has a similar training effect to the previous one. Lie on your stomach and bend your knees until you can grasp your ankles. Pull on your ankles so that your body arches. Lift your head and try to look upwards. Hold the stretched position for at least ten seconds.

● Lower yourself into a press-up position and bring your fingers together. Drop your hips until your thighs brush the floor. Look upwards and hold the stretch for at least ten seconds. You may then lift the hips clear of the mat, taking them as high as possible so that the spine curves in the reverse direction.

● Lie on your back and raise your feet up and over your head. Brace your hips with your hands, wedging your elbows against the mats. Keep your knees straight and try to touch the mat with the tips of your toes. Hold this position for as long as you can manage.

● The fifth and final exercise of this short series combines shoulder and elbow movement in a simple mobility routine. Lift both arms in front of your upper chest. Circle them one way for a while, then pause and reverse the direction of rotation.

Jiu jitsu training is exciting and it is common to finish the lesson on a 'high'. This is not a good state for travelling home; the correct thing to do is to cool down by repeating the above sequence of exercises until you feel relaxed and comfortable.

Breakfalls

You are now ready for training. But there is one more thing to work at before the lesson proper can begin; that is learning how to fall safely.

Falling is inevitable. In any self defence situation there is always a chance that you will lose your balance or be thrown to the floor (and there may not be a soft mat to land on!). Also, jiu jitsu practice involves both performing throwing techniques and having them performed on you. This means that you *must* learn how to land with safety.

Jiu jitsu uses a technique progression to teach how to fall correctly and safely. By this means, a technique is broken down into a series of stages, each one leading to the next. The purpose of this is to introduce students gradually to practice and so build up their confidence.

Side breakfall

Begin from a crouching position, extending both arms in front of you. This is the start position for all subsequent breakfalls.

Allow yourself to overbalance to the left and slap down on to the mat with your left palm (fig. 5). Your shoulder and elbow must be springy rather than rigid, while the rest of your body is relaxed. Note how the right knee is brought across the front of the groin to protect it. The right hand is ready and can be moved quickly to cover the face or body should the need arise.

When you can side breakfall effectively from this low position, gradually increase the height of your starting stance until you are breakfalling safely from a standing position. Practise breakfalling to both sides and spend extra time on the weaker side.

Fig. 5 Side breakfall ▶

Back breakfall

Back breakfall also begins from the crouching start position. Increase the starting height as you become more confident.

Roll backwards along the curve of your spine, leaning forwards to create an arched back. Bring both your arms across your body and tuck your chin into your chest. Depending on the speed of landing, you will roll up on to your shoulders, at which time you should slap down with the palms of your hands to arrest the movement (fig. 6). Bring both feet down to the mat.

Front breakfall

Begin from a crouching position and gradually increase the height as you gain confidence.

Dive forwards on to the palms of your hands, allowing the elbows to give under your weight (fig. 7). Keep your knees together to prevent an opponent's kick from the rear from reaching your groin. Turn your hands inwards so that the fingers approach each other.

◀ Fig. 6 Back breakfall

▼ Fig. 7 Front breakfall

▲ *Fig. 8 Foreflap breakfall*

Foreflap breakfall

The foreflap breakfall is used when the opponent successfully applies a stomach throw. Don't try to roll out of this particular throw because the opponent may keep hold of you; if he does, injury may well result.

Spring forwards as in the previous example, but this time tuck your chin into your chest and perform a forward roll. Bring the soles of your feet down and splay your arms, slapping them palm-downwards against the mat (fig. 8).

Rolling breakfall

Begin this technique from the crouched position and gradually increase the height until you can quite literally dive into the mat without injury. This technique also uses a rolling action along the curve of the spine and though it is in some ways similar to the previous technique, you do not slap the mat to bring motion to a stop. Consequently, skilled students often roll right over, gathering their feet under them. This allows them to spring into a fighting stance, ready to take immediate defensive action.

Drop your left palm to the floor and lean forwards. Point your right hand at your feet and lift both heels.

Tuck your head in and spring forwards on to your shoulders, rolling along the curve of your spine (fig. 9). Bring your heels under you and stand up. Turn to face the imaginary attacker and take up a fighting stance.

◀ *Fig. 9 Rolling breakfall*

Striking techniques

Striking techniques are used at various stages during the application of jiu jitsu techniques. Sometimes they are used at the beginning to distract the opponent from the main thrust of your attack. At other times they are used to strike a final blow to an opponent who has been placed in a vulnerable position.

Jiu jitsu strikes tend to be used against the body's weak spots, so a great deal of impact energy is not required.

Fist

Below the roots of your fingers at the top of your palm is a ridge formed by the underside of the knuckles. Fold your fingers down so that the tips contact it, then close the fist fully by folding your thumb across the index and middle fingers. If the fist is correctly made, a right angle will be formed by the fingers and the back of the hand.

This may be difficult to achieve at first, but you must keep working at it because a wrongly formed fist 'skins' knuckles.

Don't let your thumb poke forwards or it will catch in someone's sleeve, and do not enclose it by the fingers or it will be damaged when your fist strikes something hard. Most of the time your fist can be slightly relaxed, but always tighten it fully on impact.

In this example, the opponent has been thrown to the mat and you hold his right wrist with your left hand. Take up a long stance with your left foot leading and lever his arm across your knee. Now strike down into his temple with your right fist (fig. 10).

▼ *Fig. 10 Fist strike*

Palm heel

'Palm heel' uses the palm of the hand as though it were a fist. Curl your fingers and fold the thumb in. Flex your wrist back as far as it will go.

Throw the hand forwards with the fingers and thumb relaxed. Then as soon as the strike is about to make contact, the hand tightens and the palm heel slams home.

There are many different ways of using palm heel. One is to turn your body sideways-on to the opponent and use your left hand in a horizontal, glancing palm heel strike that rotates the opponent's head (fig. 11).

Another way is to bring your hand sharply upwards, so it strikes below the opponent's chin and forces his head back. This is particularly effective against a taller person who is standing close to you. You can also use a two-handed palm heel to strike two targets simultaneously.

Palm heel is useful for attacking bony targets because the bones of the impact area are covered by a pad of cushioning flesh.

Fig. 11 Palm heel strike ▶

16

Back fist

'Back fist' uses the back of the knuckles in a circular strike to the temple, the bridge of the nose, or the jaw. Like all circular techniques, it is difficult to block.

The punching elbow is nearer to the target and it lifts until it points directly where you want the fist to go. The hips then rotate away from the opponent as the striking arm 'unrolls' into the target. Lash out and strike with the back of the two large knuckles.

Lean into the strike and relax your elbow and wrist until just before impact; then tense them. Allow natural joint elasticity to snap the wrist back.

By turning the body *away* from the strike delivery, the shoulders open out and the full length of the arm can be used to advantage.

Use back fist in a vertical strike to the opponent's face (fig. 12).

Fig. 12 Back fist strike ▶

Hammer fist

'Hammer fist' uses the closed fist in a clubbing action.

Draw the opponent's head down with your right hand and strike on to the base of his skull with left hammer fist (fig. 13).

Use hammer fist against an opponent who is standing behind you. In this case, protect your face before looking over your shoulder. Then swing your fist behind you in an upswinging arc into the opponent's groin. Use hammer fist also in a horizontal swing to the side of the opponent's head or temple. Begin with your left foot leading and your right fist drawn back to your right ear, with the little finger side turned upwards. Then draw back your leading guard hand and turn your hips fully towards the opponent. This combination of drawing back and twisting produces a powerful strike.

Hammer fist is one of the safest strikes to use because it cushions the bones of the hand with a pad of flesh.

Fig. 13 Hammer fist strike ▶

Knife hand

Knife hand uses the little finger edge of the palm to concentrate a great deal of force over a small area. Strike with the part which lies between the base of your little finger and the wrist. Stiffen your fingers on impact to prevent them from jarring painfully together. Cup the hand slightly during horizontal circular strikes.

Here you have stepped well to the opponent's closed side, deflecting his punch with your right hand. Bring the blocking arm back to your left ear and cut back into the opponent's floating ribs (fig. 14).

You can also use knife hand in a descending strike to the opponent's collar bone. Begin with your left foot and left hand leading. Then draw back your left hand and turn your hips fully towards the opponent. Bring your right hand up and past your right ear before dropping it down on to the target.

Fig. 14 Knife hand strike ▶

Elbow strike

The elbow is a devastating weapon which is at its best in the close-up situation. Make sure you strike with the tip of the elbow, not the length of the forearm, because the former concentrates more power into the strike.

There are many different ways of making an elbow strike. In the illustrated example, draw the opponent's right arm down and twist your hips towards him so your leading foot swivels outwards. Swing your elbow in a horizontal circular action that clips the side of his jaw (fig. 15).

Use elbow strike also in an upswinging arc that catches the opponent's chin and drives his head back. Stand in left stance with your knees bent. Then draw your lead hand back and turn your hips to the front. Swing your right elbow forwards and up. Alternatively, use elbow strike against an opponent standing behind you by peeking over your shoulder to make sure the coast is clear, and then stepping back with your right foot. Drive your elbow out so it strikes the opponent in the solar plexus.

20   *Fig. 15 Elbow strike* ▶

Kicking techniques

Front snap kick

Front kick uses the thick pad of flesh that runs beneath the toes. Point your foot in a straight line with your shin and pull your toes back. It is sometimes difficult to do this correctly, so practise by placing the sole of your foot flat on the floor and then raise the heel as high as you can.

As its name implies, the kick uses a snapping action of the knee joint to thrust the ball of the foot into the target. First the knee is raised sharply until it points at the target, then the lower leg snaps out. Snap the spent kick back and lose no time in setting your foot back on the mat because it is never a good idea to stand on one leg in front of an opponent!

Keep your elbows to your side so that they don't flap about, and don't straighten your supporting leg. Take care not to move your body weight too far forwards or your spent kick will simply slap down, in easy reach of the opponent.

Take the opponent's right punch with your left hand and raise your right knee until it points at his chin. Then snap the lower leg out in a fast arc. Pull back your toes and strike with the ball of the foot (fig. 16).

Use this technique to attack the opponent's groin, solar plexus or chin, and practise delivering the kick with both front and rear legs.

▼ *Fig. 16 Front snap kick*

Roundhouse kick

Roundhouse kick uses either the ball of the foot or the instep to strike the opponent's groin, mid-section or jaw. The foot follows a rising, circular path that lifts it over obstacles. But always kick from the correct range and angle, or you may hurt your foot.

The opponent approaches from the left side. Block his right punch with your left hand while strongly rotating your shoulders to the left and lifting the right foot off the mat. Your hips then follow the shoulders, so the supporting foot swivels anti-clockwise through 90°. The flexed right knee is brought across the front of the body.

Begin straightening your lower leg as the knee turns towards the target. Strike the opponent's solar plexus with the ball of your foot (fig. 17) and withdraw the spent kick sharply. Set the foot down gently into a new fighting stance.

Relax your shoulders so that they don't hunch up, and maintain an effective guard throughout.

Fig. 17 Roundhouse kick ▶

Side kick to kneecap

Side kick uses the heel and little toe edge of the foot in a direct, thrusting attack to the opponent's knee or mid-section. Practise the correct foot shape by lifting your big toe while depressing the others.

The opponent stands with his left foot leading and punches with his right fist. Slide your leading left foot to the left and block with your right hand. Maintain an effective guard as you bring your right knee forwards and up, across the front of your body. Then thrust the heel and little toe edge of your foot diagonally downwards and into the side of the opponent's knee, allowing your supporting foot to swivel outwards (fig. 18).

Lean back to counterbalance the weight of your extending leg and pull your knee back before setting it down in an effective stance.

Fig. 18 Side kick to kneecap ▶

Back kick

Use this kick when the opponent is standing behind you. In this case he takes hold of both of your wrists. Step forwards with your left foot, lift your right knee and thrust your heel back in a straight line, into his groin or solar plexus (fig. 19). Point the ball of the foot towards the mat.

This kick is very powerful because it strikes home with the heel. If you look at the way it is used, you will see that it is effective from an early stage because the ankle of the kicking foot is brought close to the supporting knee. This means that should the opponent step in unexpectedly, you will still catch him in the groin!

On the other hand, it is definitely not a good idea to stand on one leg when the opponent has taken hold of you, so perform the kick as quickly as you can and then either turn into an effective defensive position, or open up distance between yourself and the opponent.

Fig. 19 Back kick ▶

Blocking techniques

Blocking techniques are used to prevent the opponent's punch, kick, strike or grab from succeeding. Typically you use your hand or forearm to deflect the opponent's technique. You may also need to move your body, both to evade the opponent and to power the blocking action. The following is a selection of blocking techniques used in jiu jitsu.

Inside forearm block

This technique uses the thumb side of the forearm to sweep the opponent's attack to the side. The forearm is fairly long and this means that the block has quite a depth of field, so accuracy isn't critical. Having said that, block with the forearm more or less vertical and aim to catch the opponent's technique with your wrist area.

Begin by turning your hips towards the opponent, using this action to help power the block. First drop your leading guard hand across the front of your stomach and then quickly bring it up in an action like a windscreen wiper, knocking the opponent's punch outwards (fig. 20).

Be prepared to block a second time if the opponent punches with his left fist.

Use inside forearm block to deflect attacks to the chest, face and head.

▼ *Fig. 20 Inside forearm block*

Outside forearm block

The second type of forearm block uses the little finger side of the forearm to knock the opponent's punch sideways.

The opponent faces you in left stance and punches with his right fist. Begin from right foot leading stance by sliding your right foot to the left. This turns your body into the block and makes it more powerful.

As you turn, lift your right fist to your right ear, then swing it sharply across the front of your chest and sweep the opponent's punch outwards (fig. 21).

This is a very powerful block which is effective against techniques aimed at the chest, head and face. But keep the blocking forearm vertical!

Fig. 21 Outside forearm block ▶

Rising forearm block

This block also makes use of the area below the little finger. In this case, though, the attacking technique is deflected upwards, or diagonally to the side.

Both partners stand in left stance and the opponent either punches at your face with his right fist, or attempts a descending hammer fist strike to the top of your head. Bring your left fist diagonally up and across your upper chest and face. Rotate your forearm as the technique completes and deflect the opponent's punch upwards (fig. 22).

Note that the block travels away from your body as well as upwards. This means that incoming techniques are met at an earlier stage, when they have less power. The sloping forearm also means that descending strikes tend to glance off.

Fig. 22 Rising forearm block ▶

Palm block

Palm block is extremely effective, though greater accuracy is required since the blocking area is much smaller than the forearm. Like palm heel strike, the block uses a slightly cupped palm, delivered with a thrusting action into the opponent's upper arm.

Palm block can be delivered with either the front or the rear guarding hand.

Begin with both partners in left stance. The opponent punches with his right fist. Step sharply around with your right foot to take you out of line, and deliver the block with your right hand (fig. 23). The opponent is now 'closed off': that is to say, he must first change his position before he can reach you with his left fist.

Fig. 23 Palm block ▶

Downwards/inside forearm block

This block uses the little finger side of the forearm to deflect punches and kicks to the stomach and groin areas.

Both partners take up left stance. Your opponent punches with his right fist. Pull your right hip sharply back, using this action to help power the leading left forearm downwards and along a circular path which knocks the punch outwards (fig. 24).

Block away from your body so that there is a greater margin of safety.

A correctly performed block strikes the *side* of the opponent's shin – it doesn't meet the force of his kick full on! This is an important point because the mass and energy of a fast-moving shin is easily sufficient to break your forearm! So don't strike down on to the kick; rather swing your fist into the side of it.

Fig. 24 Downwards/inside forearm block ▶

Low x-block

This block makes use of both forearms in the form of an 'x'. Begin practice by having your partner kick *slowly* and with control!

Face the opponent in left stance. The opponent attempts a right front kick. Push with your trailing right leg and slide forwards on your left foot so you go to meet the kick. At the same time, lean forwards and thrust both forearms out from your body so they cross at the wrists. Rotate your forearms until the fists turn palm-downwards, trapping the opponent's shin between them (fig. 25).

Allow your forearms to slide under the impact and this will minimise bruising when a really hard kick is blocked. Don't lean your chin too far forwards as you apply the block!

Fig. 25 Low x-block ▶

Throwing techniques

Rather than simply using brute force, jiu jitsu throws use leverage to take the opponent's centre of gravity to a position where he becomes unstable and can be toppled over.

All the following throws satisfy three important criteria:

● they are effective for a wide range of different sized people
● they need only the minimum of skill to produce a worthwhile result
● they are responses to realistic forms of attack.

Hip throw

Begin by facing the opponent, both of you in left fighting stance. He throws a punch with his right fist, leaning well forwards to develop power. Step across with your left foot, block his punch with your left arm and curl your fingers over his right biceps (fig. 26).

Fig. 26 ▶

Note the right hand held in a defensive guard in front of your face. Remember, the opponent also has a left fist! The purpose of the side step is to set up the following throw.

Curl your right arm around the opponent's back and turn strongly, pivoting on your left leg. The turn completes with your back turned fully on the opponent. The opening side step has set your feet up so you are between his. Bend your knees to drop below his centre of gravity. Draw down strongly on his right arm and hold him firmly with your right arm across his back (fig. 27).

Straighten your knees, levering him off the mat. At the same time, pull down on his right arm and roll him over your right hip (fig. 28). Drop him at your feet.

This technique works because it lifts the opponent from the mat. Provided you drop under his centre of gravity and use your thigh muscles, you will have no trouble in lifting all but the heaviest opponent.

▲ *Fig. 27*

▲ *Fig. 28*

▲ *Fig. 29*

▲ *Fig. 30*

▲ *Fig. 31*

Half shoulder

Both partners take up left fighting stance. Step forwards quickly and deflect the opponent's punch with your right hand. Lift your left hand and grasp the opponent's right wrist. Draw your right hand back and strike the opponent in the ribs with back fist (fig. 29).

Note how your body has turned until it is sideways-on to the opponent.

Slip your right arm under the opponent's. Your leading right foot is already in the correct position. Turn your back on the opponent while drawing your left foot in, until it is close to the right. Bend both knees to drop under the opponent's centre of gravity (fig. 30).

Straighten your knees and draw the opponent over your right hip (fig. 31).

▲ *Fig. 32*

▲ *Fig. 33*

▲ *Fig. 34*

Outside hock

Close in on the opponent by advancing on your left foot. Take his right forearm in your left hand and swing your right forearm across his throat. Throw your body weight forwards, so the opponent is bent back and unable to turn the tables on you (fig. 32).

Bring your right foot through and hook the heel back sharply into the opponent's spine or kidneys (fig. 33).

Drop the spent kick to the mat, placing your foot so the back of your right thigh presses against the opponent's. Sweep backwards with your right leg so the opponent is unbalanced (fig. 34). Keep hold of his right hand so he falls at your feet.

This throw works because you have taken the opponent's centre of gravity over his right leg, and then swept the latter away.

Drawing ankle

Both partners face each other in left stances. The opponent steps forwards with his right foot and throws a punch using his right fist. Block the punch with your left hand, curling the fingers over his elbow and drawing his arm down. Take the upper part of his left arm in your right hand and lift it. Swing your left foot forwards in a scooping motion to strike the front of the opponent's ankle (fig. 35). This causes the opponent to fall over his right foot.

This throw works properly when the opponent's centre of gravity has been drawn forwards and over his right foot.

You will know whether you have set the throw up correctly by the ease with which the opponent falls. It shouldn't be necessary to drag him over his foot; simply use the energy of his punching action to help draw him forwards. This, of course, means timing the throw correctly and not waiting until he realises his punch has failed and tries to withdraw it.

Fig. 35 Drawing ankle ▶

Hold down techniques

Hold downs are used to secure and control the opponent once he has been thrown. It is always a good plan to keep hold of the opponent's arm after throwing him because this prevents him from rolling away from you and taking up a defensive position. Having said that, make sure the opponent doesn't pull you down on top of him!

By keeping your hips close to the mat at all times, you will lower your centre of gravity and force the opponent to try and lever up your entire body weight. By applying leverage against his joints, you will encourage him not to make too much trouble for you.

The important factor is to be able to keep your co-ordination when you go down to the mat. Children do this with ease because they are used to tumbling about. Adults have to regain this ability.

Fig. 36 Hold down (1) ▶

Hold down (1)

In this first hold down, you have kept hold of the opponent's right arm and he has fallen at your feet. Step quickly forwards and jam your right knee into his side and your left knee into his neck. Use body weight to pin him down.

Fold his right elbow by applying pressure to the back of his wrist with your right hand. Secure the wristlock by pushing your left arm under his elbow and taking your right wrist in your left hand (fig. 36).

Drawing up his bent wrist will guarantee his compliance!

Hold down (2)

Again, you have kept hold of the opponent's right wrist after throwing him. Step over his head with your left foot, then quickly sit down close to him and lean back, levering his right arm across the front of your right thigh. Jam your right shin against his ribs and hook your left heel under his chin (fig. 37).

Control him by levering down on his straight right arm. Note the guarding position of your left hand.

Fig. 37 Hold down (2) ▶

Hold down (3)

This hold down follows on from a throw such as outside hock, where your right arm is across the opponent's throat as you throw him. Follow him down to the mat, then push his right arm to the side and trap it by encircling his neck and shoulder with your right arm. Lower your head and spread your legs wide for stability (fig. 38).

Fig. 38 Hold down (3) ▶

Locking techniques

Before going into detail about technique, I want to make a point about the way these locks are applied. This concerns the way in which they make use of the attacker's own force. The harder the attack, the more forceful the defence. Never oppose force with force because to do so means that the stronger prevails. Instead, go with the applied force, while re-directing it to your own advantage.

Straight armlock

Begin from left stances. The opponent punches to your stomach with his right fist. Knock the punch down and to the side with downwards/inside forearm block. The opponent leans forwards slightly because he has put considerable power into his punch (fig. 39).

Drop your rear guard hand and seize the opponent's spent punch before he has time to retrieve it. Guard your face with your left forearm (fig. 40). Note the position of the opponent's left fist, and be prepared for him to use it!

Spin right around on your left foot, sliding your right foot back until the two of you are almost parallel and facing in the same direction. Turn the opponent's arm palm-upwards. Loop your left arm over the top of his trapped arm (fig. 41). Perform a back elbow to the face from this position if the opponent proves a little hard to deal with.

Hook your left arm under the opponent's upper arm and lift it. Apply the armlock by pressing down on the opponent's wrist while fully extending his arm (fig. 42).

Fig. 39 ▶

Fig. 40 ▶

Fig. 41 ▶

Fig. 42 ▶

▲ *Fig. 43*

▲ *Fig. 44*

▲ *Fig. 45*

Wristlock

Each partner stands with his right foot leading. The opponent reaches forwards and pushes you in the chest with his right hand. Bring your left hand up and seize the opponent's right wrist, using an over-hand grasp. Note the position of your right guarding hand (fig. 43).

Turn the opponent's wrist until his palm faces upwards. Then bring your right hand up to reinforce the left, and press into the back of the opponent's hand with your thumbs (fig. 44). This causes his wrist to flex.

Continue to apply force to the back of the opponent's hand so that he is brought to his knees in front of you (fig. 45).

Back hammer lock

Both partners face each other in left fighting stance. The opponent punches with his right fist. Deflect the punch to the side with your left arm and raise the right hand in a hammer fist configuration. Strike the opponent's elbow with your right fist (fig. 46).

Step around with your right leg so that you are almost parallel to the opponent. Push the opponent's right wrist back as you step, and both lift and flex his right elbow. Push your left hand under his forearm until you can press directly down on his shoulder joint. Pull back your right fist in readiness for a punch (fig. 47).

▼ *Fig. 46*

▼ *Fig. 47*

Combined shoulder lock and wristlock

Both you and your partner take up left fighting stance. Your partner punches with his right fist. Respond by sliding your left leading foot diagonally forwards and blocking the opponent's punch with your right palm (fig. 48).

Step through with your left foot and take the opponent's spent punch down and to your right. Take the back of the opponent's right wrist in your right hand and apply a wristlock by flexing the joint as far as it will go. Lift the right arm, ensuring that the elbow is straight, and apply pressure to his right shoulder blade with your left arm (fig. 49).

▼ *Fig. 48*

▼ *Fig. 49*

Escape techniques

Despite your very best efforts, your opponent may well succeed in applying a lock or hold down on you. If this happens, then you need to know how to escape.

Escape from head chancery

Here the opponent has succeeded in applying a head chancery from the side-on position. Strike just above his right knee with hammer fist (fig. 50).

Step quickly through with your left foot so that it comes across the front of the opponent's. At the same time, drop your right hand down and take the front of his right upper ankle. Thrust your left hand upwards and press against his upper back (fig. 51).

Pull strongly on the opponent's right foot while pressing against his back with your left palm. His left foot is trapped by yours, so he falls forwards on to his face (fig. 52).

▲ Fig. 50

▲ Fig. 51

▲ Fig. 52

43

Escape from straight armlock

The opponent has trapped your right arm in a straight armlock (*see* again figs 39–42). Use the palm of your left hand to push his left elbow forwards (fig. 53).

At the same time, twist your right forearm until the hand faces palm-downwards. This defeats the lock (fig. 54).

Step across the front of the opponent's feet with your right leg and bend your knees so that your waist drops below his centre of gravity.

Straighten your knees and lift the opponent's feet clear of the mat. Then draw him over your right hip so he falls on to his back in front of you (fig. 55). Finish the technique with a lock or hold.

▲ *Fig. 53*

▲ *Fig. 54*

Escape from ground strangle

The opponent kneels between your legs and applies a strangle (fig. 56).

Strike him a glancing blow across the side of his jaw with your left palm. At the same time, take his right wrist with your right hand and draw your right knee up so that the sole of your foot presses against his left knee (fig. 57 on page 46).

▲ *Fig. 55*

▲ *Fig. 56*

Push his left knee and turn his right hand palm-upwards as he falls diagonally forwards. Raise your left foot (fig. 58).

Slide your left foot under the opponent's chin, pressing the sole down on his left forearm. Apply a lock to the opponent's right wrist (fig. 59).

This technique illustrates how important it is to retain your coordination and sense of purpose when you have been taken to the mat.

Fig. 57 ▶

▼ Fig. 58

▼ Fig. 59

Further reading

The only correct way to learn jiu jitsu is in a proper club under the supervision of a qualified coach. In this context, relevant, well written and well illustrated books can be very useful indeed. The following publications are strongly recommended.

● *Jiu Jitsu: The Official World Jiu Jitsu Federation Training Manual – White Belt to Green Belt.*
● *Jiu Jitsu: The Official World Jiu Jitsu Federation Training Manual – Blue Belt to Brown Belt.*
● *Jiu Jitsu: The Official World Jiu Jitsu Federation Training Manual – The Black Belt Syllabus.*

These three books are published by A & C Black. You can order copies direct from:

The World Jiu Jitsu Federation
Barlows Lane
Fazakerley
Liverpool L9 9EH.

Tel: 0151 523 9611

A wide range of inexpensive training videos is also available from this address.

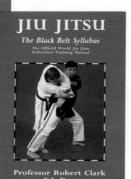

Index